# PIANO MUSIC BY WOMEN COMPOSERS

## 30 Intermediate to Upper Intermediate Level Piec

T0088846

Compiled and Edited by Immanuela Gruenberg

ISBN 978-1-70514-753-5

Copyright © 2023 by HAL LEONARD LLC
International Copyright Secured All Rights Reserved

No part of this publication may be reproduced in any form or by any means without the prior written permission of the Publisher.

Visit Hal Leonard Online at
**www.halleonard.com**

World headquarters, contact:
**Hal Leonard**
7777 West Bluemound Road
Milwaukee, WI 53213
Email: info@halleonard.com

In Europe, contact:
**Hal Leonard Europe Limited**
1 Red Place
London, W1K 6PL
Email: info@halleonardeurope.com

In Australia, contact:
**Hal Leonard Australia Pty. Ltd.**
4 Lentara Court
Cheltenham, Victoria, 3192 Australia
Email: info@halleonard.com.au

# PREFACE

Upon embarking on this project, I had little idea of what I would find. There were, of course, the "usual suspects:" women composers whose names and whose music have stood the test of time and are familiar to many. There were also those whose names ring a bell but whose music does not. The real unknowns were, well, the unknowns. How many women composers whose music is worth studying and listening to were out there? Adding to the puzzle was the fact this project took place during the COVID-19 pandemic when libraries were closed, reducing the number and type of sources I had access to. By the time I had to make the final decision on what to include in these two volumes, I had five times as much music as could be included within the allotted space. This meant that I had to leave out eighty percent of the music I had collected.

When selecting the twenty percent to be included, I searched for the following: beautiful, interesting compositions that students can benefit from and will love learning, teachers will enjoy teaching, and audiences will appreciate; a variety to styles, composers, and nationalities; showcasing as many composers as possible, while striking a balance between well-known, lesser known, and unknown composers. With these in mind, I chose mostly shorter works or, as with Marianna Martines's sonata, a single movement rather than the complete work.

*—Immanuela Gruenberg*

# CONTENTS

# COMPOSER BIOGRAPHIES

French composer **Mélanie Bonis** (1858–1937) studied organ with César Franck, and harmony with Ernest Guiraud at the Paris Conservatoire. She married in 1883 and for about ten years devoted herself to raising a family. Bonis composed over 300 works, about half of them piano compositions, the others organ, chamber, choral, and orchestra works. Most of her music was published during her lifetime. In 1907 she became a member of the committee of the *Société des compositeurs de musique* and from 1910 to 1914 served as its secretary.

Born in Paris, **Cécile Chaminade** (1857–1944) was a successful pianist and composer. She studied privately with Félix Le Couppey, Marmontel, and Benjamin Godard. She composed mainly character pieces. These were very successful both with audiences and financially. She toured France, was a favorite of queen Victoria, and in 1908 she toured the United States, performing in 12 cities. In 1913 she became the first female composer to be granted admission to the Order of the Legion of Honor. Of her approximately 400 compositions, almost all of which were published during her lifetime, the majority are piano works. The rest are songs, an opera, a ballet, and orchestral suites. Her compositions were enormously successful with both critics and audiences.

**Fredrikke Egeberg** (1815–1861) was a Norwegian pianist and composer. She was the youngest of nine children and the only daughter. Several of her family members, including some of her siblings, became professional and amateur musicians. She composed piano music, songs, and choral works.

**Louise Farrenc** (1804–1875) was a French composer, pianist, scholar, and teacher. She studied piano with a student of Clementi and later with Ignaz Moscheles and Johann Nepomuk Hummel. At age fifteen she entered the Paris Conservatoire to study composition with Anton Reicha. In 1821 she married flutist Aristide Farrenc with whom she collaborated in concerts and in her research. He also published her early compositions. These received high praise from Schumann in his *Neue Zeitschrift für Musik*. In 1842 she was appointed Professor of Piano at the Paris Conservatoire, a position she held until 1873. Many of her students won competitions and became professional musicians. In an effort to revive 17th and 18th century music, she and her students organized and performed concerts featuring that music. Her research on that topic was published in *Le trésor des pianists*. She composed mainly for the piano, but also chamber works, choral music, and symphonies. In 1845, her piano etudes became required repertoire at the Conservatoire.

Danish composer **Emma Hartmann** (1807–1851) composed under the pseudonym Frederik H. Palmer. She was married to Emilius Hartmann who came from a German-origin Danish family of musicians. Emma Hartmann's first published composition was originally composed for a Student Association dance. Later publications included 22 *Romances and Songs*. In 1908, a collection of her piano pieces was published by her son, Frederik Hartmann.

English composer and pianist **Cecile Hartog** (1857–1940) was born in London. She studied music at the Royal Academy of Music, London, as well as in Berlin. She composed and published songs, piano, and chamber pieces. Her Summer Song appeared in 1891.

**Marie Jaëll** (1846–1925), also known by her maiden name, Marie Trautmann, was a French pianist, composer, and pedagogue. She studied with Ignaz Moscheles, Heinrich Herz, and Franz Liszt, and started preforming at a very young age. At twenty she married pianist Alfred Jaëll, with whom she performed and who apparently also helped with her career. She was a successful pianist, and the first French pianist to perform the complete Beethoven piano sonatas. Saint-Saëns dedicated to her his first piano concerto and the *Etude en forme de valse*. Her compositions were published and were well received. As a pedagogue, Marie Jaëll developed a method of playing based on her scientific analysis of how the muscles work.

Her aim was to make technique and artistry work synergistically, combining technical elements with artistic ones. In addition, she encouraged performers to develop the ability to create a mental image of the sought-after sound. Her method became known as The Jaëll Method.

**Natalia Janotha** (1856–1932) was a Polish pianist and composer. She started piano lessons with her father, later studying in Berlin with, among others, Brahms and Clara Schumann. She concertized from a young age. Janotha lived about 30 years in London where she was a favorite with audiences and with the nobility, receiving the Victoria badge and Diamond Jubilee commemoration medal from Queen Victoria. Natalia Janotha was also court pianist for Emperor Wilhelm of Germany. Through personal contacts with Chopin's relatives she had access to part of his estate which enabled her to contribute to research on Chopin. Her compositions number about 400 works.

Born into an artistic family, **Josephine Lang** (1815–1880) was a German composer. She began her piano lessons with her mother, an opera singer. She later studied theory with Felix Mendelssohn. Felix and his sister, Fanny, were enthusiastic about Lang. In 1838, Robert Schumann wrote a glowing review of one of her songs in his *Neue Zeitschrift für Musik*. Ferdinand Hiller helped get her music published. She composed primarily songs (about 150), but also piano pieces and some choral works.

English composer and pianist **Kate Loder** (1825–1904) was born into a musical family. She entered the Royal Academy of Music in London at age 13, studying the piano with Lucy Anderson and composition with Charles Lucas. She started performing in public at a young age. In 1844, at 18 years of age, she became the first female professor of harmony at the Royal Academy. Upon her marriage to Sir Henry Thompson she stopped performing in public but continued to compose and to teach. Brahms' *Deutsches Requiem* received its English premier at her house, with her and Cipriani Potter playing a duet version of the orchestra part. Kate Loder composed piano, organ, chamber, and orchestral works.

**Marianna Martines (Anna Katharina Martinez)** (1744–1812), was an Austrian composer, pianist, and singer of Spanish-Italian descent. As a child she was educated by Metastasio, who lived in the same house as she and her family. From a young age she enjoyed great success as both pianist and as singer. She studied with Haydn, who, like Metastasio, lived in the same house, and with Johann Adolph Hasse. In 1773 she became an honorary member of the Bologna Accademia Filarmonica. She often performed at the Austrian Imperial Court and ran soirées that were attended by the likes of Haydn and Mozart. She composed various vocal works and several keyboard sonatas.

**Emilie Mayer** (1812–1883) was a German composer. She started her musical education at a young age but began serious composition studies relatively late. She studied with Carl Loewe in Stettin and later, in Berlin, she studied fugue and counterpoint with Adolf Bernhard Marx and orchestration with Wilhelm Wieprecht. In spite of that late start, she produced a large number of compositions, including symphonies, piano sonatas, chamber works for various ensembles, and works for piano solo. She traveled a great deal, organizing concerts to promote her music which was performed in many European cities. She also served as Associate Director of the Opera Academy in Berlin.

German pianist and composer **Fanny Mendelssohn** (1805–1847) was born into a highly educated, respected, and wealthy Jewish German family that later converted to Protestantism. She was the granddaughter of the Enlightenment philosopher Moses Mendelssohn. Her remarkable musical talent, evident already at a young age, was nurtured by her family that included a long line of educated women, with an emphasis on music education. Alongside her brother Felix, she studied piano and composition with Ludwig Berger and Carl Friedrich Zelter, as well as with Marie Bigot. In 1820 both siblings joined the Berlin *Sing Akademie*. Fanny was one of nineteenth century's most prolific women composers and most gifted pianists. In an 1824 letter to Goehte, Zelter wrote that Fanny had already composed 32 fugues. A very gifted pianist, praised by Ignaz Moscheles and others, she performed mainly at the Mendelssohn family's Sunday concerts. A lifelong proponent of the works of Bach, Beethoven, and Felix Mendelssohn, she composed small-scale piano pieces, chamber works, cantatas, organ works, choral works, vocal solo songs, duets, trios, quartets, and various arrangements.

German pianist and composer **Adele aus der Ohe** (1861–1937) studied with Theodor Kullak and, from age twelve to age nineteen, with Franz Liszt. In 1886 she made her American debut playing Liszt's first piano concerto. She performed Tchaikovsky's first piano concerto at the inaugural concert at Carnegie Hall, with Tchaikovsky conducting. After many years in the United States she returned to Germany in 1906. She composed mainly solo piano works and songs.

**Delphine von Schauroth** (1814–1887) was a highly successful German pianist and composer. She started piano lessons at age seven and studied with Friedrich Kalkbrenner in Paris. At age ten she went on her first concert tour. That was followed by more tours. Felix Mendelssohn met her in Munich and wrote to his sister, Fanny, that von Schauroth composed a passage for his G minor piano concerto "that makes a startling effect." He did not, however, mention, where that passage is. Mendelssohn dedicated the concerto to her. In an 1839 letter to her brother, Fanny Mendelssohn describes von Schauroth's "extraordinary talent" and her "inspired improvisations."

**Fanny Scholfield Petrie** (presumedly 1859–1933). At the time of printing, almost no information regarding this composer's life and training were found. This dearth of information will hopefully change.

**Clara Schumann** (1819–1896) was a German pianist, composer, and teacher. She was one of the leading piano virtuosos of the 19th century and the teacher of many professional pianists. She started piano lessons with her mother Mariane, herself a gifted singer and pianist who had appeared as solo singer, and was the piano soloist in John Field's second piano concerto at the Leipzig Gewandhaus. When, following her parents' divorce, her father Friedrich Wieck gained full custody, she studied with him, receiving a thorough musical education in a highly disciplined environment. Wieck Schumann toured from a young age and continued concertizing into her sixties, playing solo recitals, chamber concerts, and as soloist with orchestras. At 21, and against her father's wishes, she married Robert Schumann, whose works she later edited for Breitkopf & Härtel. Her compositions include a large number of solo piano works as well as lieder, concertos, chamber music, and arrangements.

**Anna Stubenberg** (1821–1912) was born in Austria to an old noble family. Her father was Count Gustav Adolph von Stubenberg. She grew up in Pest, Hungary, where she studied music, art, and languages. She was known as a gifted improviser. She composed short piano pieces such as dances and marches and Lieder.

**Maria Szymanowska** (1789–1831) was a Polish composer and virtuoso pianist in 19th-century's virtuoso-rich Europe. She toured extensively throughout Europe, enjoying great success with audiences, critics, and with the European nobility. In 1827 Maria Szymanowska settled in St. Petersburg, where she continued to perform, teach, compose, and where she ran a salon that attracted influential musicians and poets, among them Goethe, Cherubini, and Rossini. She composed primarily for the piano. Her compositions include dances (mazurkas, polonaises, waltzes), nocturnes, marches, vocal works, and some chamber works.

**Stephanie Vrabély (Countess Stephanie von Wurmbrand-Stuppach)** (1849–1919) was an Austrian pianist and composer of Slovak descent. She started piano lessons at an early age. Through her family she met Brahms, Liszt, and Tausig, who became her teacher. At age 14 she published a collection of thirty songs. After her marriage she settled in Vienna, where her music was performed by leading musicians. She gave concerts in several European cities and promoted the first performances of Bartok's music in Vienna and in Manchester. She composed a large number of piano works. These include character pieces, dances, concert pieces, and a sonata.

# Grand Spanish Waltz in A Major

Mélanie Bonis
(1858–1937)

Fingerings are editorial suggestions.

Copyright © 2023 by HAL LEONARD LLC
International Copyright Secured All Rights Reserved

* These fingering markings appear in the souce.

63
mf
69
75
4
3 2 1
80
86
sf
risoluto
91
3

96
101
legg.
106
crescendo
111
ff
mf
sostenuto
116
122

128
134
140
146
p legg.
151
156

161
f
167
173
179
p legg.
ff risoluto
184
crescendo
189
ff risoluto

194
199
204
crescendo
209
214
ff
tr
220
allargando

*to Madeleine Verger*

# It's Raining!

Mélanie Bonis
(1858–1937)

Fingerings in parentheses are editorial suggestions.

Copyright © 2023 by HAL LEONARD LLC
International Copyright Secured All Rights Reserved

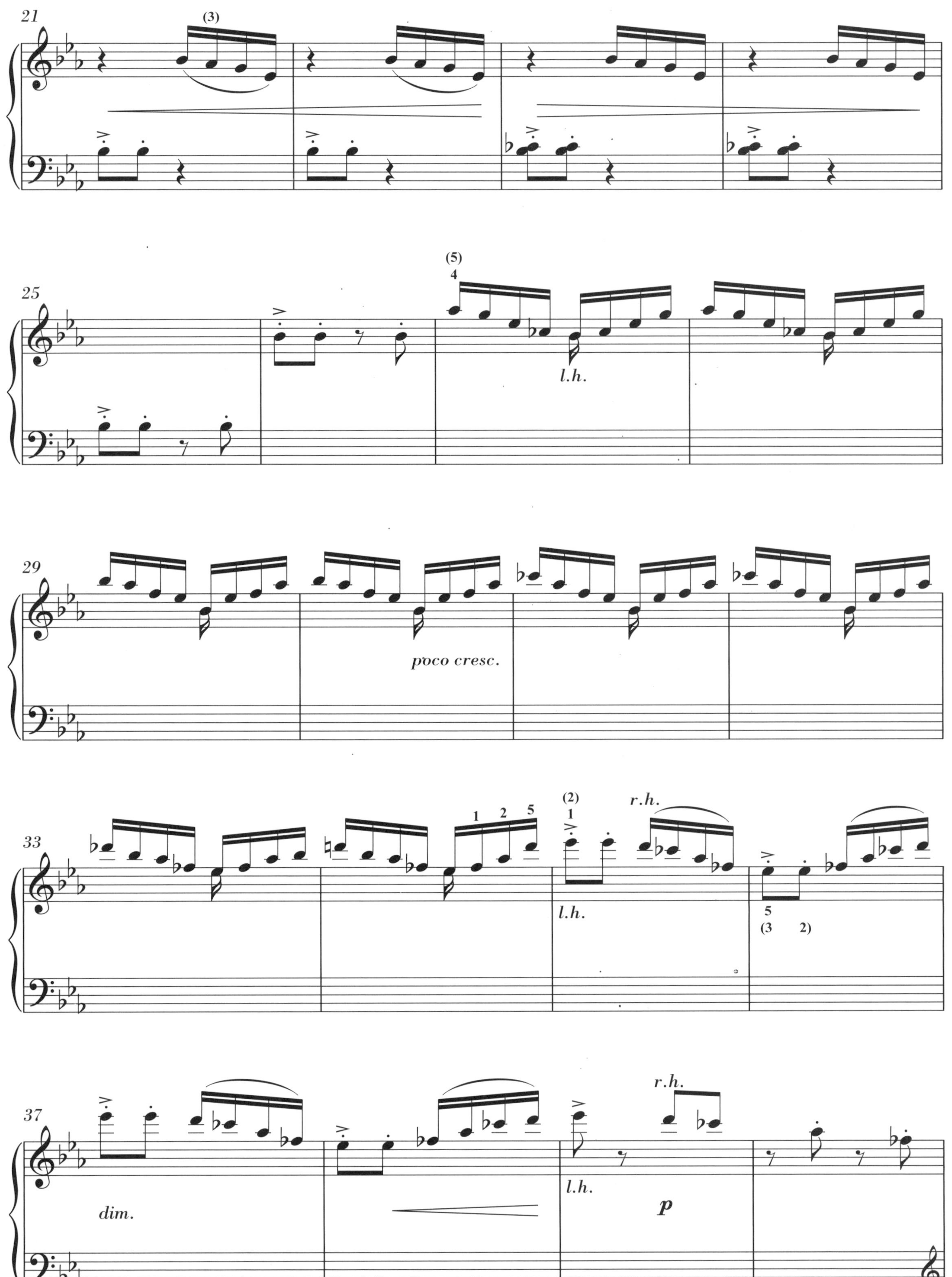
21
(3)
25
(5)
4
l.h.
29
poco cresc.
33
1 2 5
(2)
1
r.h.
l.h.
5
(3 2)
37
dim.
r.h.
l.h.
p

41
ff
dim. molto
(3, l.h. above)

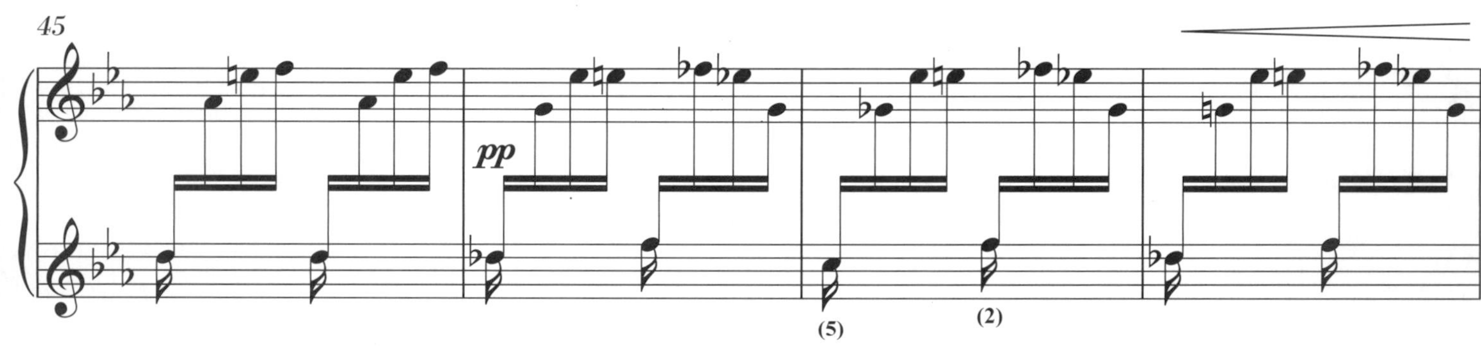
45
pp
(5)
(2)

49
pp

53
(1/2)

58
rit.

63
cheerfully
a tempo
68
cresc.
p
73
f
pp
p
legg.
78
l.h. over
cresc.
mf
83
p

88
l.h.
r.h.
rit.
mp [a tempo]
93
97
cresc.
101
dim.
105
pp

109
(3)
113
p
117
cresc.
121
ff
dim. molto
125
(4)
(3)
p

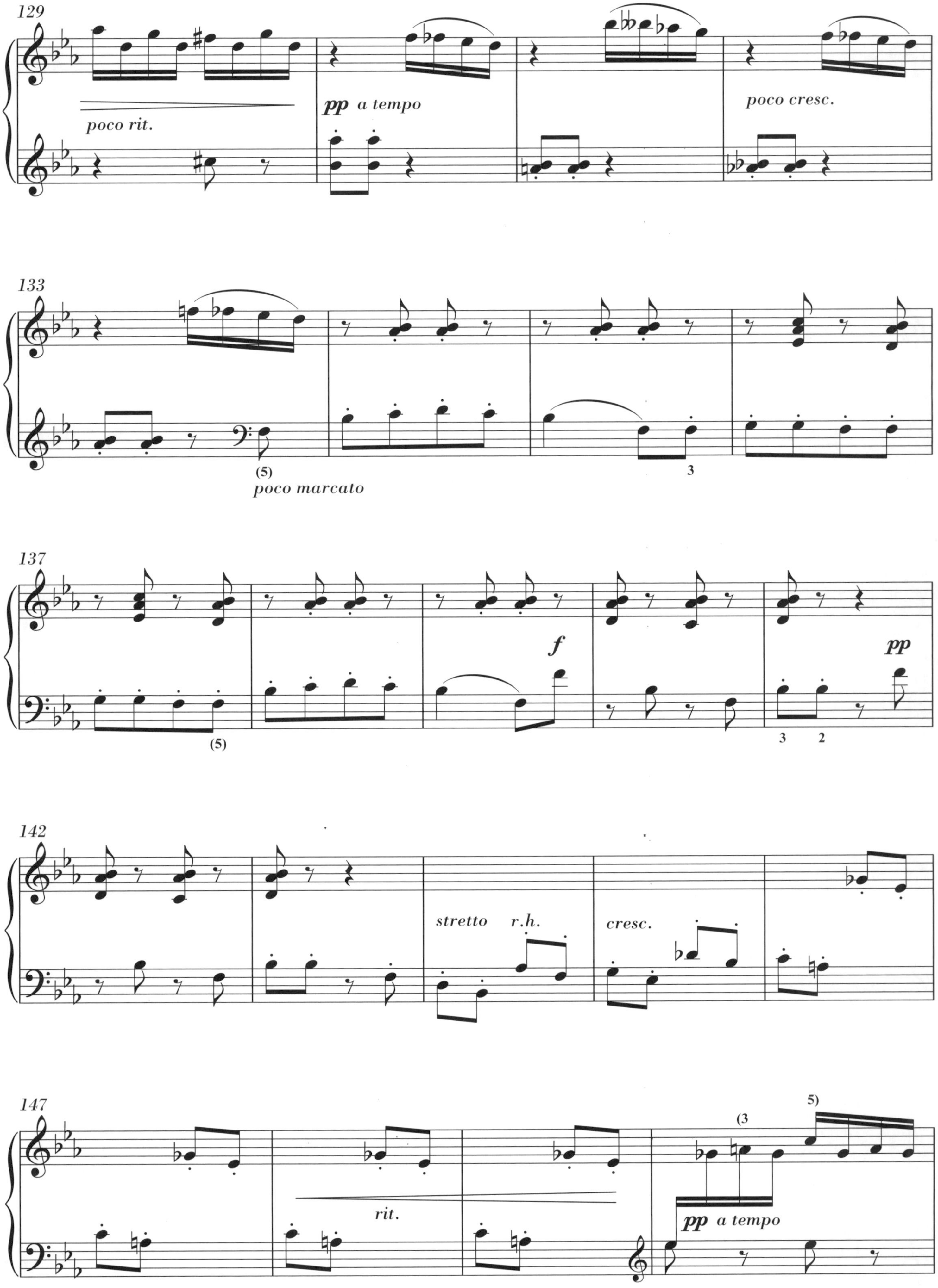
129
poco rit.
pp a tempo
poco cresc.
133
(5)
poco marcato
3
137
f
pp
(5)
3 2
142
stretto r.h.
cresc.
147
rit.
pp a tempo
(3
5)

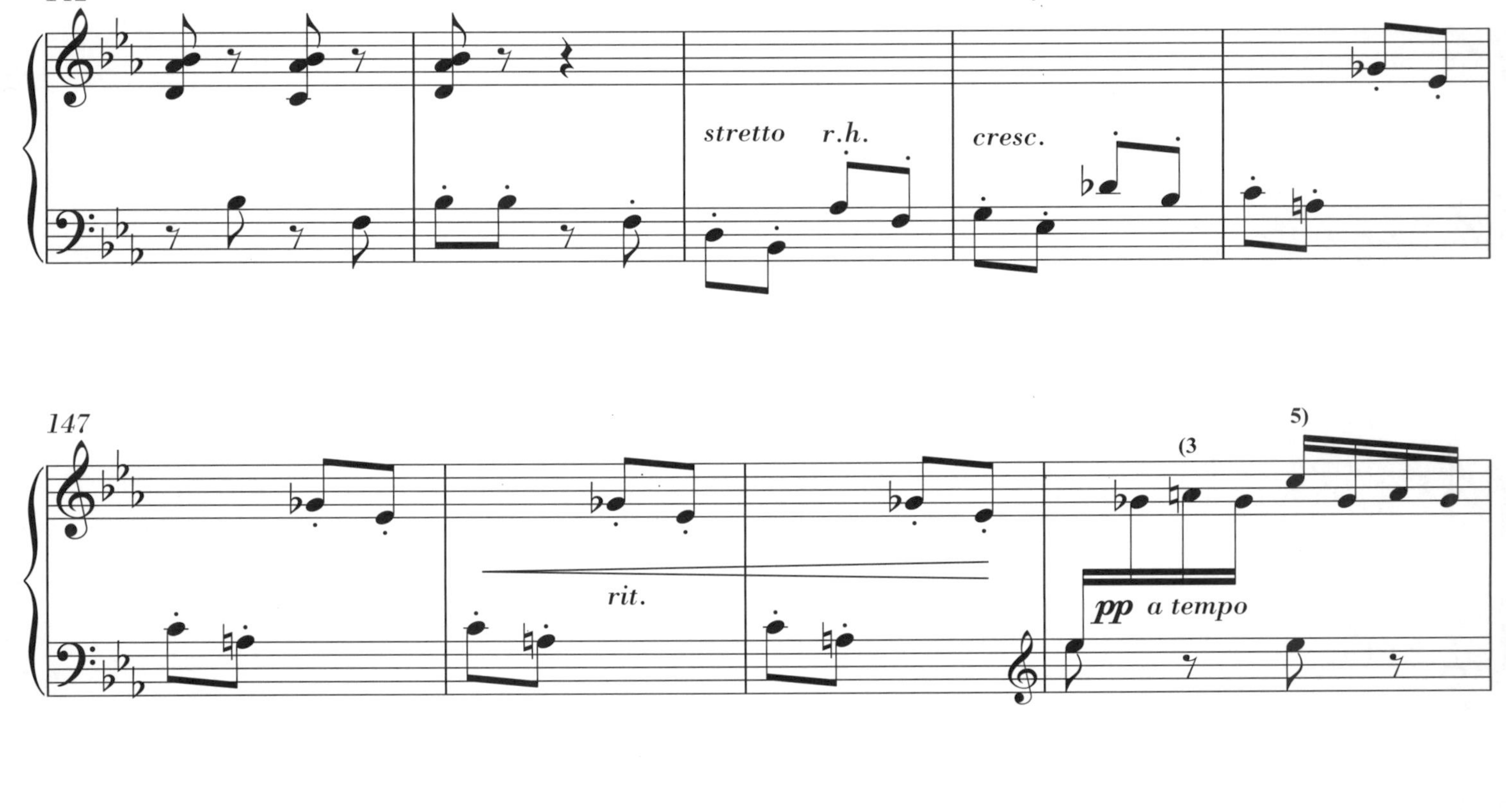

151
155
(2 3)
cresc.
159
4
163
rit.
p stretto
168
p
8va
(l.h.)

*to Rolande Beaudouin*

# Little Waltz in B-flat Major

*Children's Album (Volume 2)*, Op. 126, No. 12

Cécile Chaminade
(1857–1944)

Fingerings are editorial suggestions.

Copyright © 2023 by HAL LEONARD LLC
International Copyright Secured All Rights Reserved

20
dolce
a tempo
24
cresc.
28
32
cresc.
f
36
dim.
p rit.

40

*mf a tempo*

*cresc.*

44

*f* *rit.*

49

*a tempo*

(1)

53

*poco rit.*

*mf a tempo*

(1)

58

*cresc.*

63
f
rit.
p
a tempo
(1)
68
f
73
77
p
81
1
1
3
f

*to Henriette Chaminade*

# Melancholy

## *Two Pieces*, Op. 25, No. 1

Cécile Chaminade
(1857–1944)

Fingerings are editorial suggestions.

Copyright © 2023 by HAL LEONARD LLC
International Copyright Secured All Rights Reserved

12
dolcissimo
poco rit.
15
f a tempo
marcato
poco string.
cresc.
l.h.
r.h.
18
p
rit.
dolcissimo
21
f a tempo
dim.
(l.h.)
(r.h.)
24
mf
p
pp

27
dim.
pp
placato
30
33
dim.
36
mf
dim.
pp
39
poco rit.
dolcissimo

# Song Without Words in E-flat Major

*Six Songs Without Words for Piano*

Fredrikke Egeberg
(1815–1861)

Fingerings are editorial suggestions.

Copyright © 2023 by HAL LEONARD LLC
International Copyright Secured All Rights Reserved

# Etude in F Major

*25 Intermediate Studies*, Op. 42, No. 5

Louise Farrenc
(1804–1875)

**Allegretto** 𝅗𝅥. = 80 [𝅗𝅥. = 60]

Fingerings in parentheses are editorial suggestions.

Copyright © 2023 by HAL LEONARD LLC
International Copyright Secured All Rights Reserved

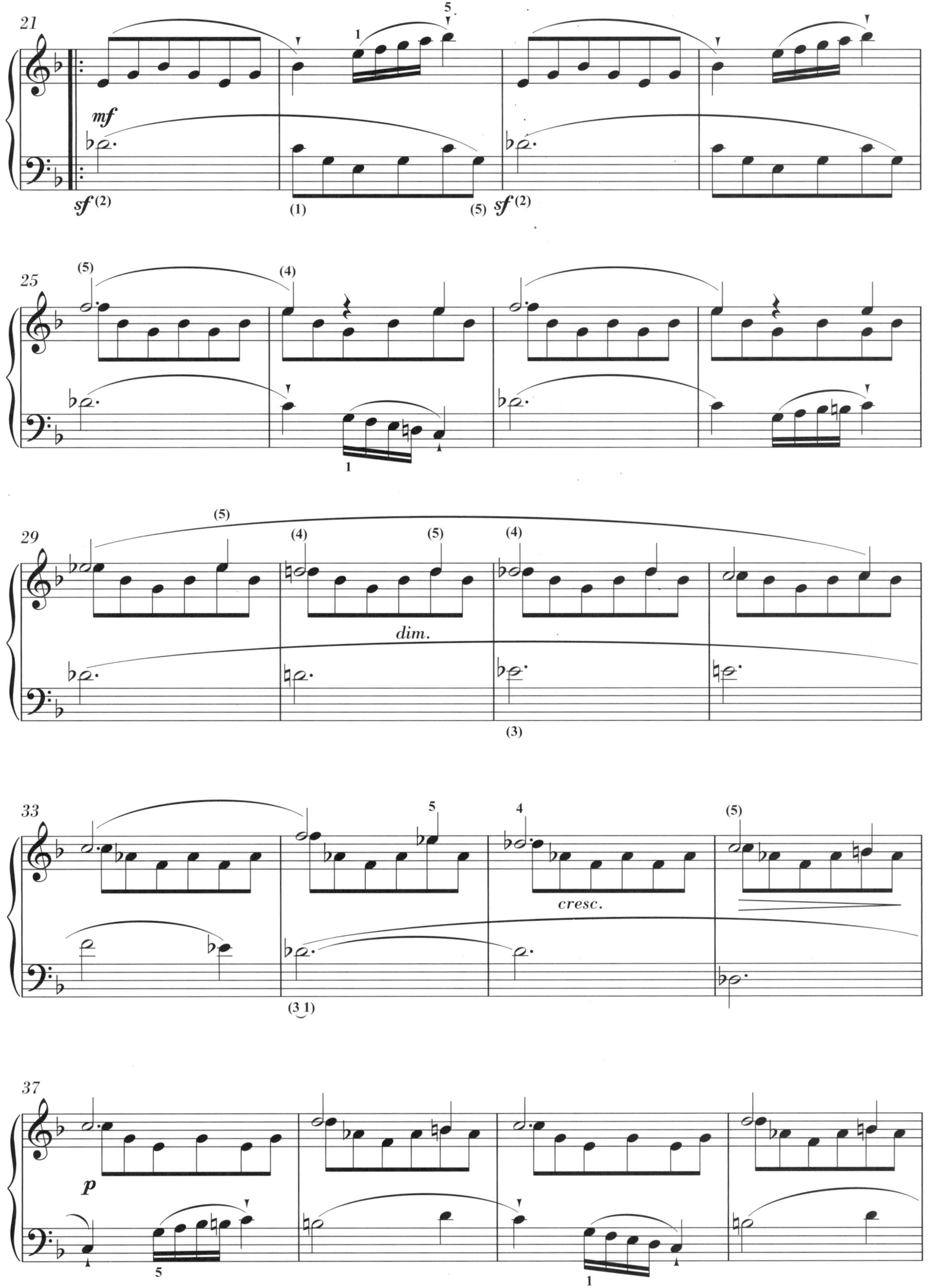
21
mf
sf (2)
(1)
(5)
sf (2)
25
(5)
(4)
29
(5)
(4)
(5)
(4)
dim.
(3)
33
5
4
(5)
cresc.
(3 1)
37
p
5
1

41

*cresc.*

*poco riten.*

45

*a tempo*

50

55

*cresc.*

*p*

60

# Etude in G Major

*12 Studies in Dexterity*, Op. 41, No. 2

Louise Farrenc
(1804–1875)

Fingerings are editorial suggestions.

Copyright © 2023 by HAL LEONARD LLC
International Copyright Secured All Rights Reserved

* These finger markings are in the source.

* These finger markings are in the source.

# Melody in A-flat Major

Louise Farrenc
(1804–1875)

Fingerings are editorial suggestions.

Copyright © 2023 by HAL LEONARD LLC
International Copyright Secured All Rights Reserved

18
p
22
cresc. e stringendo
f
26
pp
mf
30
pp
cresc.
34
dolce

38
42
cresc.
46
p
cresc.
50
dolce
54
pp

# Homesickness

*Three Piano Pieces*

Josephine Lang
(1815–1880)

Fingerings are editorial suggestions.

Copyright © 2023 by HAL LEONARD LLC
International Copyright Secured All Rights Reserved

26
1.
2.
f espress.
cresc.
31
pp
dim.
p
f
36
p
stringendo
f
rit.
pesante
f
40
ff
dim.
pp
p espress.
rit.
p espress.
rit.
Tempo primo larghetto non troppo
44
cresc.
f

49

*f* *dim.* *pp* *p* *f* *rit.*

54

*p a tempo* *p* *cresc.*

59

*f* *p* *crescendo*

64

*f stringendo* *ff*

69

*pp dim.* *espress.* *rit.*

**Tempo più mosso**

*p*

# Minuet: Sadness

*Three Piano Pieces*

Josephine Lang
(1815–1880)

Fingerings are editorial suggestions.

Copyright © 2023 by HAL LEONARD LLC
International Copyright Secured All Rights Reserved

(24)
pp
f
30
dim.
leggiero
36
f
p
pp
41
Trio
cantando
legato
2 1 2
(3 2 1)
45
sempre legato
3
3 2

49

53

1.

57

2.

61

cresc.

*f*

dim.

65

*pp*

*p*

69
fz
rit.
73
rit.
cantando
a tempo
rocking
77
81
85

89
93
pp leggiero
97
f
p
leggiero
101
f
dim.
106
pp
pp
fz
p

110
4
pp
f
115
cresc.
pp
leggiero
119
f
p
124
128
3
1
f
p

# Piano Piece in A-flat Major

*Piano Pieces*, Op. Posthumous, No. 4

Emma Hartmann
(1807–1851)

Fingerings are editorial suggestions.

Copyright © 2023 by HAL LEONARD LLC
International Copyright Secured All Rights Reserved

21
1.
f
ff
2
25
2.
Fine
p
30
2
35
cresc.
40
f
1.
2.
D.C. al Fine

# Summer Song

Cécile Hartog
(1857–1940)

Fingerings are editorial suggestions.

Copyright © 2023 by HAL LEONARD LLC
International Copyright Secured All Rights Reserved

13
poco rit.
16
p
[a tempo]
mf
ben marcato la melodia
20
24
8va
pp
28
(8va)
mf
poco rit.
8va

32 (8va)

*mf* *a tempo*

*p*

35

*cresc.*

38

*f*

*dim.*

*p*

41

44

*cresc.*

48
rit. molto
a tempo
52
espressivo
55
58
dim.
62
8va
calando
r.h.
l.h.
(l.h.)

# Friendly Teasing
*The Good Days*

Marie Jaëll
(1846–1925)

**Cheerful but a bit sentimental [♩ = 112–126]**

Fingerings are editorial suggestions.

Copyright © 2023 by HAL LEONARD LLC
International Copyright Secured All Rights Reserved

21

*pp*

*molto rit.*

25

*a tempo*

*cresc.*

*dim.*

30

*rit.*

*a tempo*

35

40

# The Shepherd and the Echo

*The Good Days*

Marie Jaëll
(1846–1925)

Fingerings are editorial suggestions.

Copyright © 2023 by HAL LEONARD LLC
International Copyright Secured All Rights Reserved

12
3
16
3
3
4
20
24
3
3
3

# Whispers of the Forests

*The Good Days*

Marie Jaëll
(1846–1925)

**Very charming** [♩. = 100–116]

*p*

*con pedale*

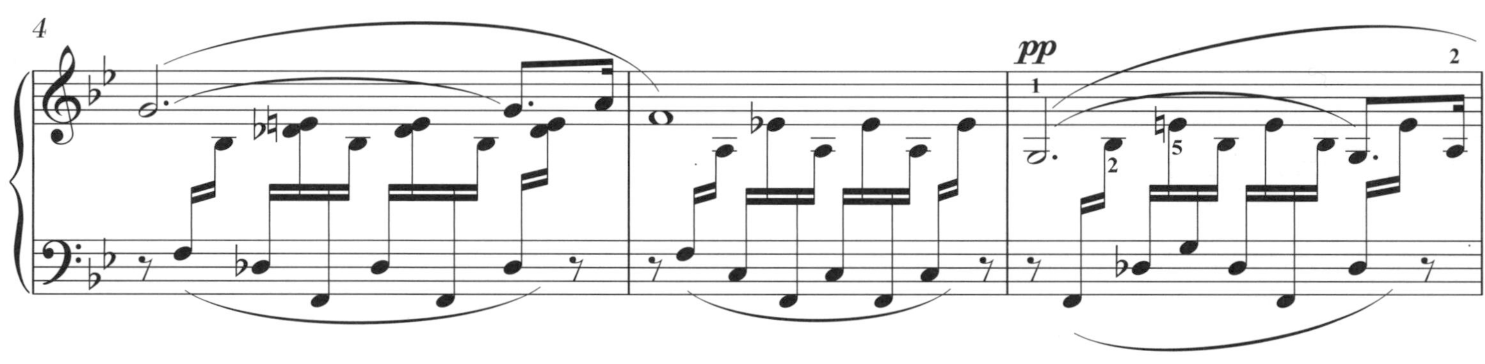


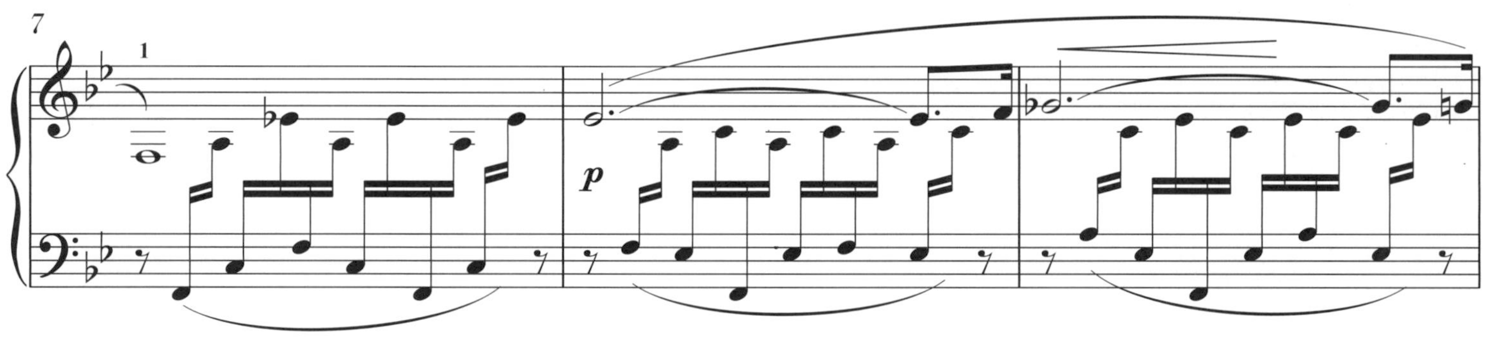


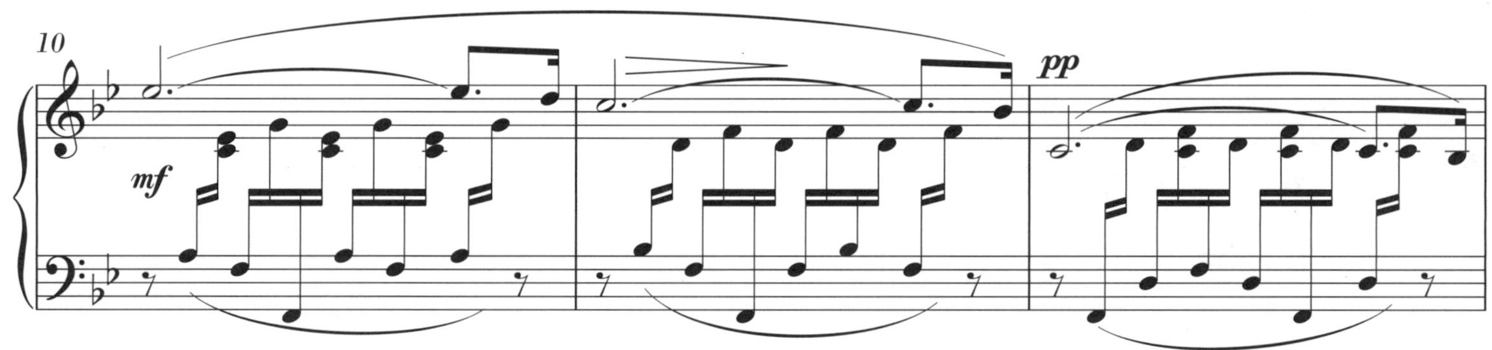


Fingerings are editorial suggestions.

Copyright © 2023 by HAL LEONARD LLC
International Copyright Secured All Rights Reserved

13
cresc.
2

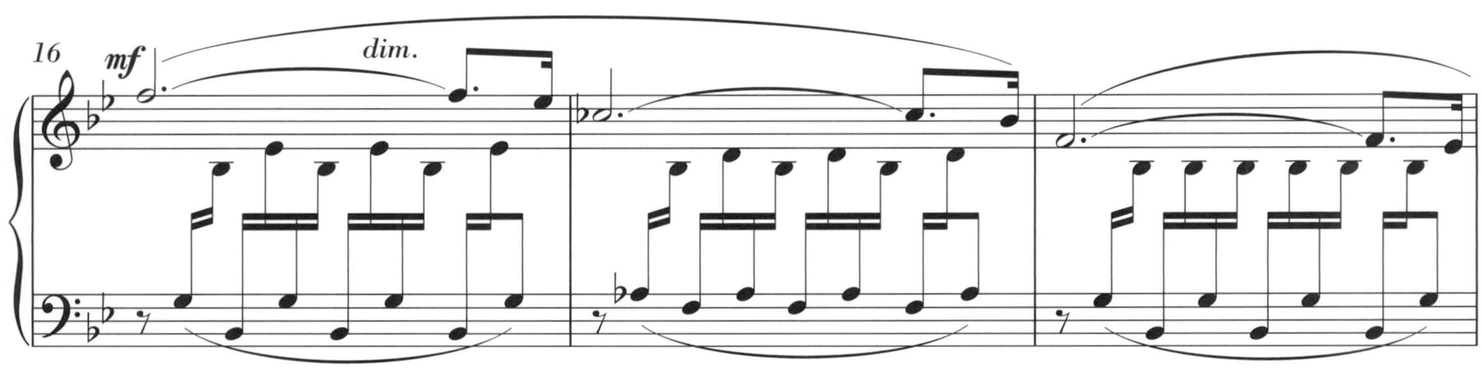
16
mf
dim.

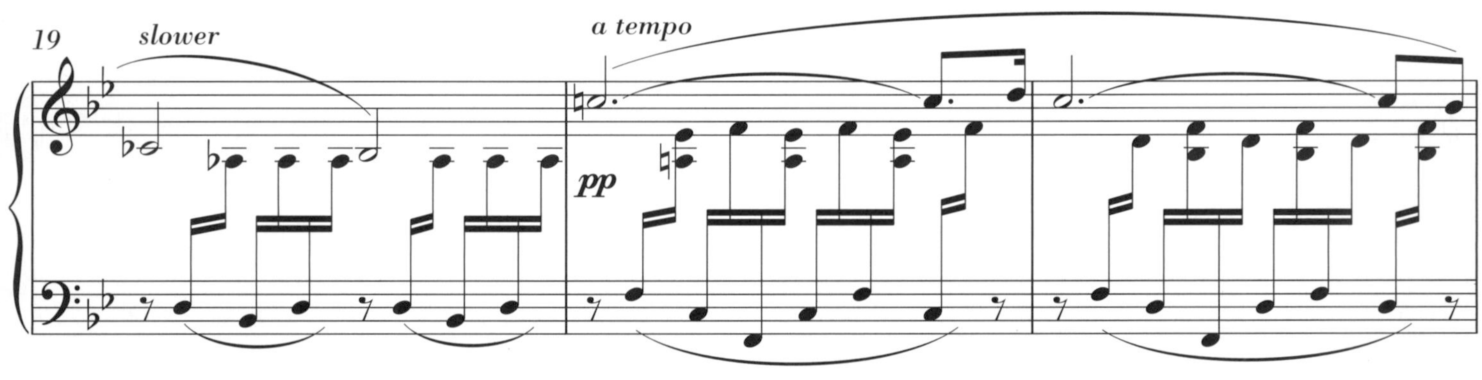
19
slower
a tempo
pp

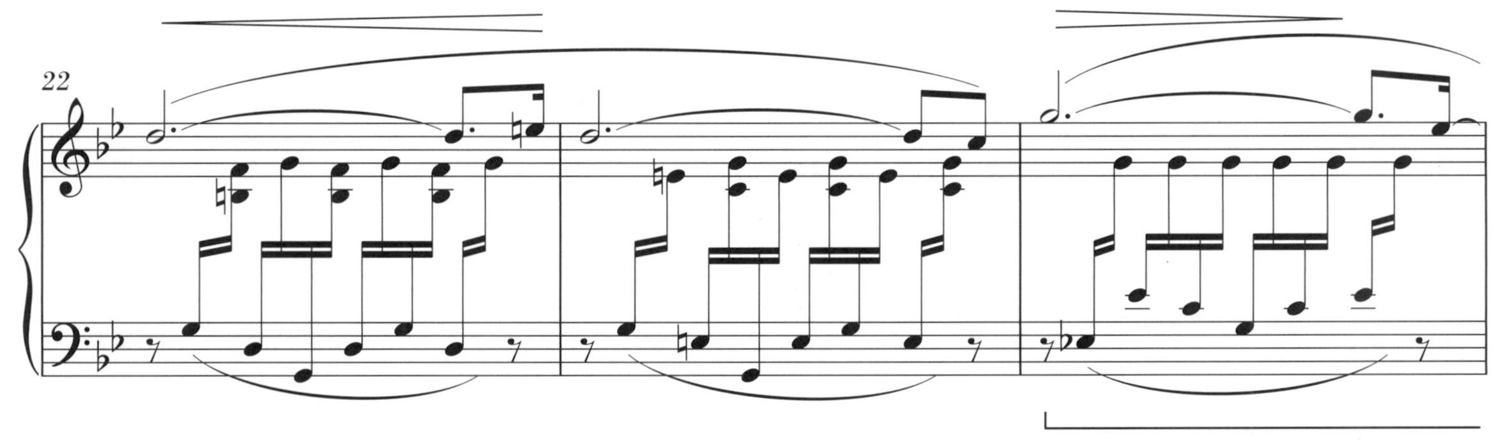
22

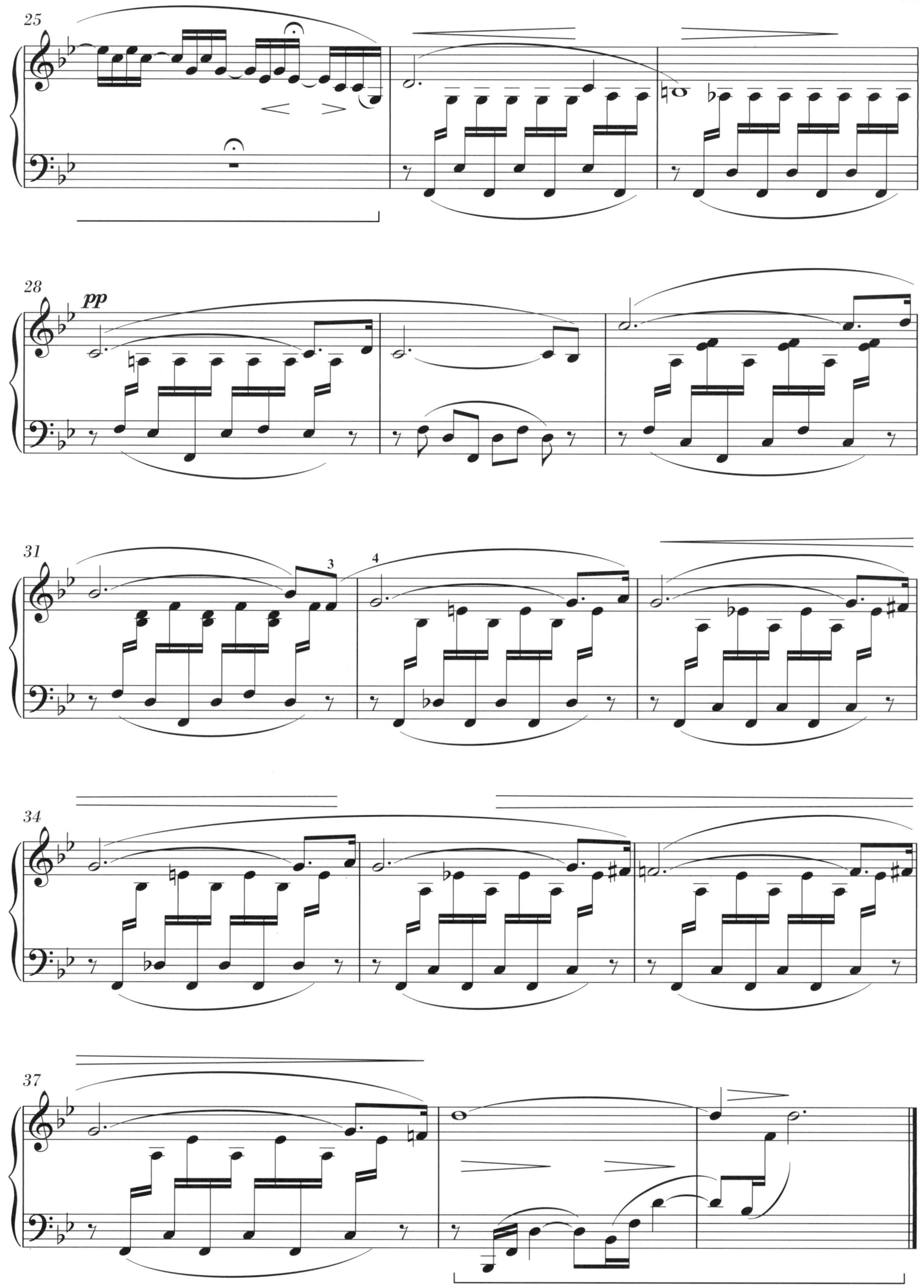
25
28
pp
31
3
4
34
37

*Dedicated to Madame Schumann*

# Edelweiss

Natalia Janotha
(1856–1932)

Fingerings are editorial suggestions.

Copyright © 2023 by HAL LEONARD LLC
International Copyright Secured All Rights Reserved

21
25
29
f
33
p
36
largamemente
p

40
pp
44
sfz
48
52
mf
mf
56
pp

60
5
4
1
4
5
2
(1)
64
p
cresc.
68
cresc. e accel.
72
f
rall.
76
a tempo

79

p

rallen.

82

p a tempo

86

90

mf

cresc.

94

p

98
sfz
accel. poco
102
p
pp
106
p
p
110
114
p
pp
l.h.

# Mazurka in A minor

Kate Loder
(1825–1904)

Fingerings are editorial suggestions.

Copyright © 2023 by HAL LEONARD LLC
International Copyright Secured All Rights Reserved

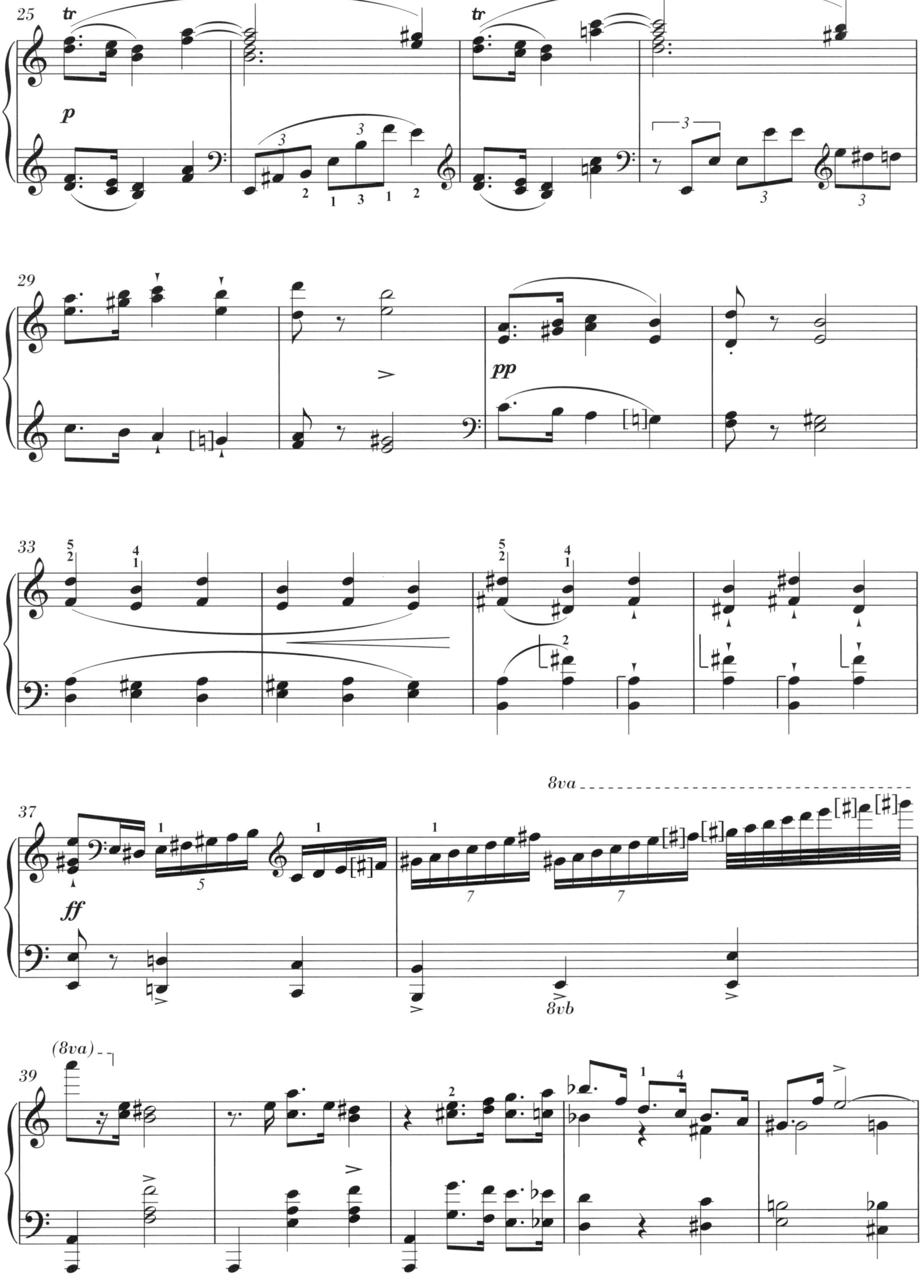
25
tr
p
29
pp
33
37
ff
8va
8vb
39
(8va)

44
p
49
53
p
58
f
62
tr
tr
p

66
68
73
78
83

88
93
ff
98
8va
p
102
pp
tr
8va
tr
ff
106
8va
8va

# Impromptu in A-flat Major

Op. 44

Emilie Mayer
(1812–1883)

Fingerings are editorial suggestions.

Copyright © 2023 by HAL LEONARD LLC
International Copyright Secured All Rights Reserved

13
sf
p
8va
16
p
19
22
25
dolce

29
32
un poco rall.
p a tempo
35
39
sf
cresc.
sf
42
sf
f
dim.

45
dolce
49
un poco rall.
53
p a tempo
57
cresc.
sf
61
sf
sf
f

64

*sf*

*p*

67

*p*

70

73

*p legato*
*un poco rall.*

76

*p*

*sf*

# Allegro
## Sonata in A Major

Marianna Martines
(1744–1812)

Fingerings are editorial suggestions.

Copyright © 2023 by HAL LEONARD LLC
International Copyright Secured All Rights Reserved

9
1
6
3
6
3
tr
6
3

11
6
3
tr

13

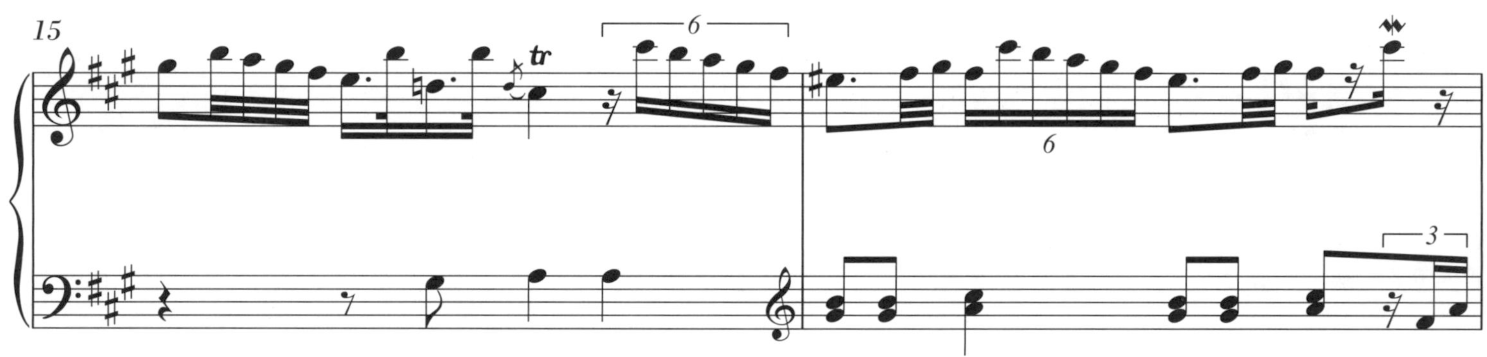
15
6
tr
6
3

marcato

27
29
31
33
35

# Larghetto

*Four Songs for the Piano*, Op. 8, No. 3

Fanny Mendelssohn
(1806–1847)

Fingerings are editorial suggestions.

Copyright © 2023 by HAL LEONARD LLC
International Copyright Secured All Rights Reserved

21
cresc.
25
p
cresc.
29
cresc.
dim.
33
p
cresc.
f
f
37
p

# Melody in E-flat Major

*Six Melodies for the Piano*, Op. 5, No. 6

Fanny Mendelssohn
(1806–1847)

Fingerings are editorial suggestions.

Copyright © 2023 by HAL LEONARD LLC
International Copyright Secured All Rights Reserved

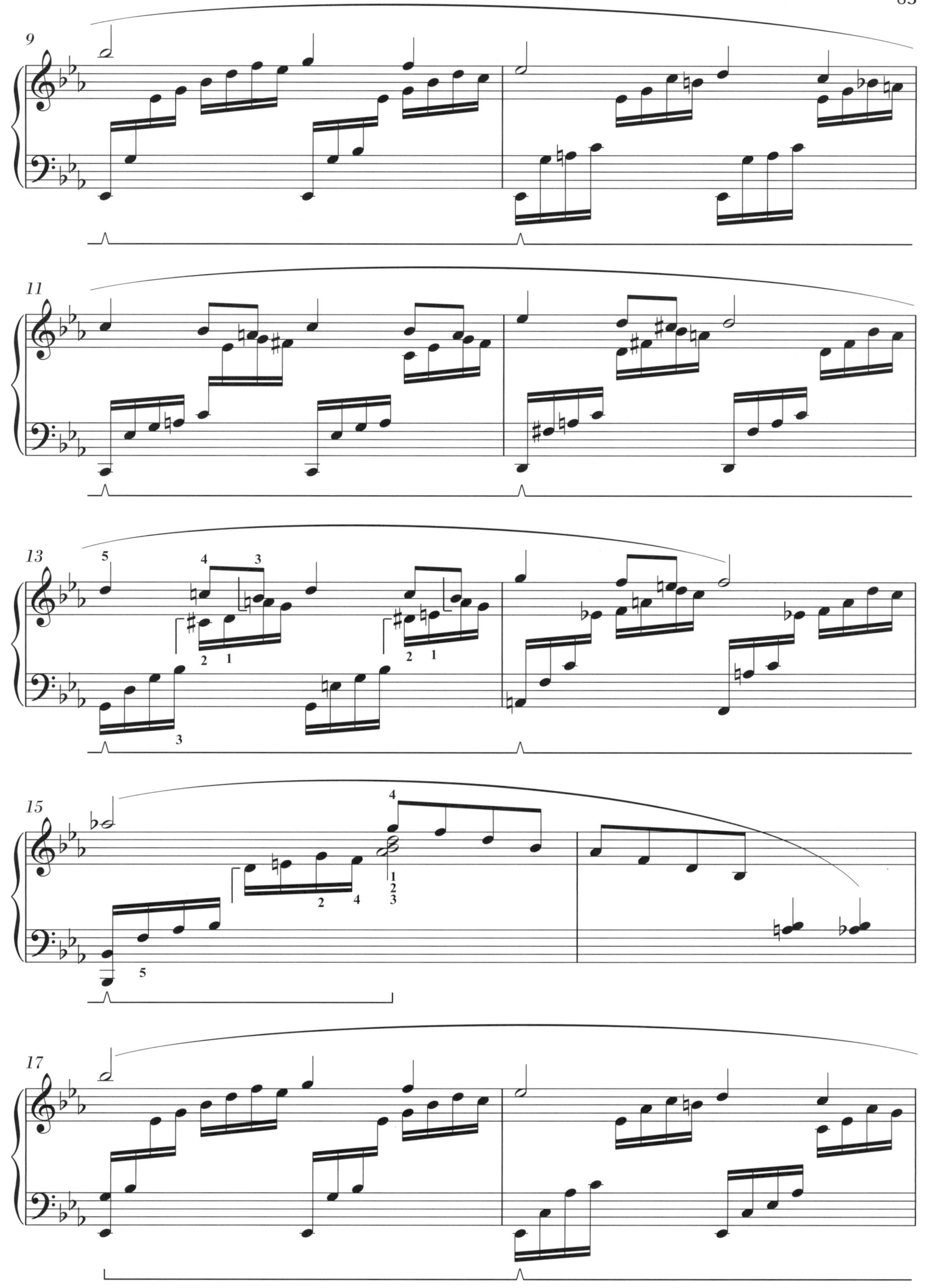
9
11
13
5
4
3
2
1
2
1
3
15
4
1
2
3
2
4
5
17

19
21
23
25
3
4
5
2
1
4
27

29
f
31
[♮]
[♭]
32
[♭]
33
[♭]
35
37
5
4
3
2
1
2
1
1
2
3
5
dim.

39
cresc.
41
[♭]
[♭]
f
43
f
[♭]
[♭]
45
[♮]
p
47

49
51
53
55
cresc.
f
dim.
57
f
dim.
f
dim.

59
61
f
rit.
a tempo
p
una corda
63
65
pp
67
8va

# A Legend

*Four Piano Pieces*, Op. 9, No. 1

Adele aus der Ohe
(1861–1937)

Fingerings are editorial suggestions.

Copyright © 2023 by HAL LEONARD LLC
International Copyright Secured All Rights Reserved

animando poco a poco
cresc.

37
dim.
mf
41
calmando
dim.
l.h.
Tempo I
45
l.h.
rit. e dim.
lunga
pp
49
sempre molto p
52
pp
p
poco marcato la melodia
poco rit.

# Sorrow

Fanny Scholfield Petrie
(presumedly 1859–1933)

Fingerings are editorial suggestions.

Copyright © 2023 by HAL LEONARD LLC
International Copyright Secured All Rights Reserved

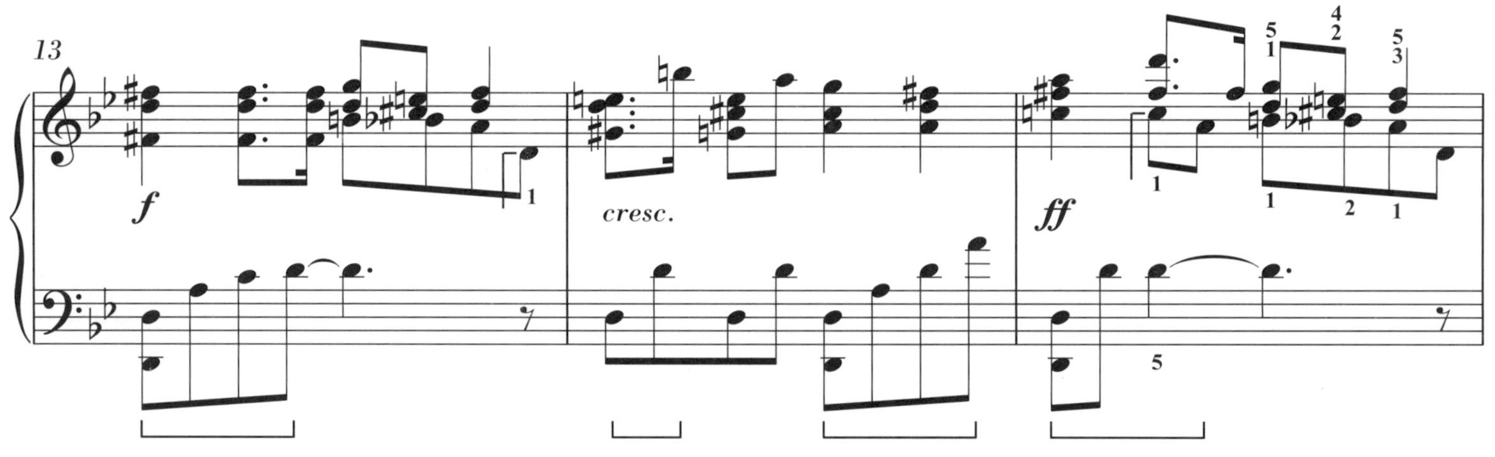
13
f
cresc.
ff

16
dim.
rall.
p
a tempo primo

19

22
rall. e dim.

# Joy

Fanny Scholfield Petrie
(presumedly 1859–1933)

Fingerings are editorial suggestions.

Copyright © 2023 by HAL LEONARD LLC
International Copyright Secured All Rights Reserved

17
p
21
cresc.
cresc.
25
f
28
cresc.
ff
31
dim.
pp

34
pp
37
cresc.
cresc.
f
41
dim.
rall.
45
p a tempo
49
non rall.
rall.

# Song Without Words in E minor

from *Six Songs Without Words*, Op. 18, No. 4

Delphine von Schauroth
(1813–1887)

Fingerings are editorial suggestions.

Copyright © 2023 by HAL LEONARD LLC
International Copyright Secured All Rights Reserved

9
p dolce
ff
11
p
dim.
13
pp con tenerezza
più molto
15
accel.
cresc.
17
ff
f
dim.

19
a tempo
con grandezza
ff
21
23
25
con fuoco
ff
ff
3
3
sf
27
8va
ff
ff
ff
8vb

# Romance in A minor
## WoO 28 (1892 version)

Clara Schumann
(1819–1896)

Fingerings are editorial suggestions.

Copyright © 2023 by HAL LEONARD LLC
International Copyright Secured All Rights Reserved

16
mf
p
20
cresc.
f accel.
24
rit.
p
somewhat animated [♩ = 72–80]
p
28
31

34
cresc.
37
cresc.
accel.
40
dim.
calando
tranquillo
pp
43
46
p
f

49
rit.
p
52
56
p
60
mf
64

67

*mf*

*p*

71

*f*

*accel.*

74

77

*calando*

*dim.*

*dim.*

80

*morendo*

# Austrian Dance in A-flat Major

*The People of Kapfenberg*, Op. 67, No. 5

Anna Stubenberg
(1821–1912)

Fingerings are editorial suggestions.

Copyright © 2023 by HAL LEONARD LLC
International Copyright Secured All Rights Reserved

# Pensée musicale

Stephanie Vrabely
(1849–1919)

Fingerings are editorial suggestions.

Copyright © 2023 by HAL LEONARD LLC
International Copyright Secured All Rights Reserved

20
24
29
34
pp
rit.
38
a tempo
tr
42
pp
tr
grazioso

# Polonaise in E minor

*18 Dances in Different Genres*

Marie Szymanowska
(1789–1831)

Fingerings are editorial suggestions.

Copyright © 2023 by HAL LEONARD LLC
International Copyright Secured All Rights Reserved

Trio
17
20
24
sf
sf
27
30
D.C. al Fine

# Quadrille in F Major

*18 Dances in Different Genres*

Marie Szymanowska
(1789–1831)

Fingerings are editorial suggestions.

Copyright © 2023 by HAL LEONARD LLC
International Copyright Secured All Rights Reserved